Nubian Goats as Pets

Nubian Goats: facts and information.

Care, health, training, play, costs and where to buy all included.

by

Elliott Lang

Published by IMB Publishing 2014

Acknowledgements

I would like to thank my children for inspiring me to write this
book. Their love and devotion for our
nubian goats made me want to share the
joy of keeping these pets with the world.

Additional thanks must go to my wife, whose patience
with me knows no bounds.

Table of Contents

Table of Contents

Introduction

Nubian goats are great animals to keep, either as pets, companion animals or as an alternative dairy option. They are both entertaining and very useful. They do fantastic work keeping the lawn cropped and keeping other animals company. They produce good quality milk without having to be mated every year. And they gambol about happily being all too cute for words.

A Nubian goat is also a fantastic addition to an existing herd, being strong and of good temperament and having a calming influence on their peers and herd mates. They also make a good basis to cross from and have a good, wide gene pool.

The decision to keep any animal is a big one and you need to be informed. You kneed to know about any special housing requirements. You need to know what they eat and if they call for any dietary additions. You need to know about any potential breeding complications. You need to know the benefits of owning them too, and make sure that there are many pros and it's not just a massive list of cons.

What you need at this stage of the game is information. This book will tell you all you need to know in order to make the rest of this decision.

Chapter 1 Nubian goats

Just look at that face! This is what initially attracts most people to the breed, and then the more people learn about their temperament and milk yield, the more appealing the Nubian becomes.

One of the other reasons that people choose Nubian goats is if they have neighbours. They are fairly quiet when provided with food, water and shelter and are generally only vocal for a cause. Nubians are such clever beasts; it's quite amusing to watch as they learn.

Once shown the proper way of doing something, for example being let out of their pen to be milked and where to stand, a Nubian will walk to the right place on their own, jump up and wait to be milked. Being full of milk can be quite uncomfortable and they know that the people help it to feel better.

7

The females have a short, glossy coat, and one of its most attractive features is the variety in colour. All coat colours are permissible; chestnut, fawn, black, white or cream. Many colour combinations are found, which give some very pretty mottled, marbled and tortoiseshell coats.

It is a breed that improves with age and there are many examples of healthy females breeding successfully and milking well even at 12 or 13 years old. Many are productive and renowned for their fruitfulness, as twins, triplets or quadruplets are common when the dam is well managed.

The Nubian goat is one of the heaviest and tallest breeds of goat, with males weighing up to 140Kgs and females up to 110Kgs. The males have a longer, thicker and wirier coat than is found in the females. They also have more convex noses than the females, which stick out more.

Males will show the same upright standing position and variety in colour as the females, although first time goat owners generally only have females, or perhaps females with a male kid at foot.

This breed does really well with heat, as they originated in North Africa. This means that they're a great source of food in the third world, and their high milk yield means they can provide protein.

Due to its strong genes, calm temperament general adaptability all over the world, the Nubian goat is a success. It has been successfully crossed with native goats of most countries to raise either the milk yield or meat production, or both.

Anglo-Nubian

This isn't really a cross as such, because "Anglo-Nubian" is the name given to the mixture of British breads and Indian and African breads that make up the Nubian goat.

Saanen

The Saanen goat is a very good milk producer, averaging at a very high yield, and although their butterfat is lower, there is more milk produced. This makes the Saanen a great goat for producing milk.

They are very beautiful to look at too, having lovely pale blond to white hair, big, inquisitive eyes, and short, proportionate legs. Saanens have shorter, pointier ears than the Nubians, and while the ears aren't as cute, they are more practical for cleaning and grooming purposes.

Saanen goats are better suited to the cold than the Nubian, as they originate in cooler, northern climes. This makes them well suited to northern Europe and the northern United states.

Nubian-Saanen

Saanen goats are quieter and can have a slightly higher yield than Nubians, and the cross Saanen-Nubian (or Snubians as many owners call them) is a fantastic cross.

Nubians have a high butterfat but the Saanen is a higher producer and is quieter. So this cross tends to be calmer and better on the stand for being milked. These are large boned, more confident and so less flighty goats.

The main benefit of the Snubian cross is the temperament and adaptability. They are also cheaper to buy than pedigrees.

Pygmy

Pygmy goats are incredibly popular pets and have a fantastic way about them. People keep pygmies as they are smaller and more compact, but still have a cheeky outlook that you'd expect from a goat. They are really sweet and an excellent option if you have limited space or want to have a couple of milk producers at the same time but *don't* want masses and masses of milk.

Pygmy goats are very good producers for their size, producing up to 2 gallons a day at the peek of their season. The milk is sweet and thick.

Pygmies are very disease resistant and have excellent health in general. They are hardy and cute. There are lots of fantastic reasons for having pygmy goats, but if you want to get the most out of a dairy animal, a Nubian is still the best bet.

Health benefits of Goats

There have been ideas for years that pets are good for your health. Stroking a cat or dog has a soothing affect and the responsibility of pet ownership has a generally stabilizing effect on mood and behavior. Studies have shown that owning a pet can increase the levels of endorphins in the brain and can increase physical health, improve sleep patterns and stave off illness. Pets can reduce the symptoms of depression. The soothing, repetitive action of stroking a pet has been proven to lower blood pressure.

How do Nubian goats fit in with this?

Because of the closeness of the bond between a Nubian goat and their owner, the love and affection shown can seriously improve ones mood.

If you find yourself becoming isolated, pets, especially less common ones, are really good icebreakers. By joining an owners' forum and going to meets and shows you can find that you have a network of friends across the world.

Pets can really push you to social interaction in ways that you are never going to be negatively judged. Owning an animal can be a great and unusual thing to have in common with people, and joining forums and going to goat shows with people can help you to make connections with people in a low pressure environment.

The depth of the bond between a Nubian goat and it's owners means that they make great companion animals.

It's strange, but even when you struggle to take care of yourself emotionally, having something dependant who relies on you to get out of bed and feed and cuddle "can help give you a sense of your own value and importance", according to Dr Ian Cook, director of Depression Research (UCLA).

The uncomplicated nature of the bond between a Nubian goat and their owner can be a great antidote to complex family and social relationships.

Having a routine with your Nubian goat can add structure to your day and this is a fantastic way to keep your mental health on track.

There are also lots of health benefits to switching from cows milk to goats milk, as, though it has a higher fat content, the fat is more digestible than that of cows milk.

There are also a lot of benefits to drinking fresh milk over pasteurized, as a lot of the vitamins and minerals are damaged during the pasteurization process. It also makes a lot of the calcium in milk difficult to absorb, while at the same time making the sugars more easily absorbed. This means that pasteurized milk not only doesn't give us all the calcium that we think it does, but it doesn't let the body feel full for as long as it should.

Milk, produced in the home, is generally not going to be pasteurized, but heat treated. Heat treated milk is far better for you. A cow will generally produce too much for a single family, but goats are just right.

There are a few questions you need to ask, though. A Nubian goat can live for up to 15 years and they need constant attention.

How many?

Goats need to live in a herd, but the herd doesn't need to be a traditional herd of goats. It is cruel to keep a goat on their own and they will quickly become unwell. A lonely goat may even stop producing milk. You don't need a whole herd of them, other animals will do. They can live in any herd type, with sheep, horses or, ideally other goats. They can't really cope on their own and need companionship.

Can you afford it?

They can be very costly, not just in the initial outlay on the animal itself but the feeding and housing requirements also need to be taken into consideration. As well as this you may need to lay out for medical expenses, (vet bills, medicine and travel to and from the vets if they're not close)

Can you cope with a grumpy/huffy goat and keep up the daily handing and fussing to get them back to their sweet old self? If your goat is a dairy goat, she will need you to continue to milk her twice daily, even if she stops liking you or you fall out.

Will you be available to clean the housing out often enough?

You need to clean them out completely and change all of their bedding and litter every week, including making sure their toys are clean. You'll also need to do a spot clean every day, taking out any obvious soiling and wet bedding.

Do you have enough space for a goat?

They need a large space to move about in. Just because they are smaller than other livestock does not mean that they can be kept in a small yard. They need access to grazing, as well as a space they can be kept away from ground that is too lush. They also need access to somewhere indoors where they can be out of the weather, such as a shed, barn or even a stable.

Can you make the commitment to milk then twice a day?

Goats need to be milked twice a day in order to keep them in milk. They need to be milked twice a day to be comfortable too. It's not fair to leave them without milking them.

What would you do if they bit you?

Could you cope with the idea that your lovely cute baby has hurt you on purpose? While the bite may not be vindictive, it can really hurt your feelings when something you have nurtured and loved breaks the trust and snaps at you. If this happens you need to be able to pull yourself together and get on with making your goat safe again. This can only happen if you remain calm and collected. Being in control of yourself can be hard if you are distressed by your pet.

Can you meet their dietary requirement?

They need grain, access to pasture and a varied diet of vegetables and leaves. They need a constant supply of fresh water, too.

The downside

There is a downside to every story, and there are difficulties with Nubian goats – as with any goats.

They are noisy, though Nubians are quieter than most. You need to be aware of any neighbours you might have. If they live close to your house and they aren't deaf you need to really think about how fair it would be on them to keep goats.

They can smell awful. Seriously, an ill or badly kept goat can smell like week old unwashed socks. If you keep them clean, then there shouldn't be a problem, but if you don't you'll need a strong stomach.

They need tending to every day. Your whole live changes when you have livestock. You can't just nip over and stay with family at Christmas without making provisions for the goat to be milked. This makes any kind of social life or holiday plans very hard.

Ask any goat owner - they'll tell you it's all worth it.

Chapter 2 Goats in the wild

Goats are incredibly adaptable creatures and can survive very well in the wild. They are fantastic browsers and can find food almost anywhere. They can be a pest in places, as they will strip the bark off trees like deer if they can't find enough grass feed.

When we think of goats in the wild, we always think first of mountain goats. With their distinctive, sharp horns and beautiful short, white coat, they are very striking to look at. They have strong, broad shoulders and strong legs. The tail is short and the snout is long and straight.

Mountain goats aren't biologically goats, but they are, for all intents and purposes, goats. They look like goats. They move like goats. They behave like goats and apparently taste like goats.

They can climb steep accents that even the most well equipped human climbers would balk at.

They are so well suited for climbing steep, rocky slopes with pitches exceeding 60°, with inner pads that provide traction and cloven hooves that spread about to make the hold stronger. They even have dewclaws like dogs and cats have, to stabilise them.

They can jump up to 12 feet in one go. The males are very aggressive to one another. The most common cause of death among mountain goats is murder. They knock each other off their purchase and push each other down cliffs. Male mountain goats will almost all fall to their death at the hands, or horns, of another goat.

Both males and females have beards, short tails, and long black horns. The males are very tall, standing at about a meter, and are about 30% heavier than the females, making violent encounters very dangerous.

In the wild, goats will live in large herds, for both protection and companionship. There can be as many as 500 does and kids in a herd. Males will tend to be solitary, avoiding each other wherever possible, and only joining with the females when they are in oestrus.

Any large predator will see goats as potential prey, and depending on where they live there can be some very frightening things out there in the dark. This accounts for the need to be nimble and fast.

Males will often fight very aggressively in breeding season and these conflicts can occasionally lead to injury or death, but are usually harmless. To avoid fighting, an animal may show a posture of nonaggression by stretching low to the ground.

The females will generally only fight to protect themselves and their young. And they can fight ferociously. Nanny goats have been known to take out cougars, lions and wolves, though bears are a different story.

Because of their amazing adaptability and tolerance for change, goats are found all over the world. The success of the Nubian breed means that in most places that you find goats, you find Nubians.

Most of the goats found wandering about in the wild tend not to be true wild goats, but feral populations of domesticated goats. There are true wild goats, such as mountain goats etc, but the majority of 'wild' goats are feral.

A lot of country parks and native animal reserves will have a section for wild goats. There will be a wild, grassy area with boulders and goats.

The problem with the success of goats is that when they become feral, they become a problem. Goats adapt really well. Environments don't adapt so well to goats, though.

Goats are excellent at finding food. They can strip entire grasslands and trees. They can kill trees, devastate crops and decimate native grazing populations by eating all the food.

Chapter 3 Choosing your goat

You're getting yourself a Nubian goat, so you need a healthy one. Getting a sick goat is bad for you and the goat, so don't do it. To avoid getting an ill goat, look for general signs of health.

The goat should be alert and lively, and it should move easily, without limping or acting stiff or sore. It should have firm, pellet poo. Be sure that it has no abscesses, and of course you'll want a well-shaped udder and teats on a milking doe. Check the feet for muck and splits.

Before you get your goat, make friends with some friendly goat owners on one of the forums. These people are knowledgeable and usually closer than you may think. They will be able to advise you on goats for sale near you, and may even accompany you to help check out your prospective new goat if you ask nicely.

Of course, you won't bring a goat home until it has a place to stay and something to eat.

1. Where to get goats

Choosing where to get your goat can be as important as choosing the goat itself. The main thing to consider is what you want from your animal. The information in this part of the book is fairly general, and you'll be able to find more specific information on where to get your goat locally to you from local goat owners. I strongly recommend joining forums and other online communities to get advice and support on specific things local to you.

a) Auctions

Livestock auctions are not for the faint hearted. If you choose to go down this route with your first goat, it is a good idea to have someone with you who knows about them. If you're friendly with a vet, that would be ideal, but if not, try to make friends with a goat owner local to you, or from one of the forums. Buying a goat at auction has a lot of risks associated with it and you really shouldn't consider this for a first goat.

Most auction animals are from big herds or are otherwise destined for the dinner table. This means that they could have all manner of health and psychological problems that would not have been picked up on.

b) Breeders

There are all sorts of arguments in favour of getting your goat from a breeder. Breeders often have lots of advice and will usually offer excellent aftercare. Local breeders will be able to advise you on things like feed suppliers, veterinary services and farriers. Goats born in captivity are better adjusted to life in captivity. Being able to trace the lineage of a goat will mean you can avoid any congenital diseases.

Professional breeders

Professional breeders are often breeding for industrial scale agriculture, but they will usually sell to the general public. Because of the high turnover of animals, though, you shouldn't expect personal attention or masses of after sales care, though they will have fantastically detailed advice for you that you should pay attention to if you do choose to go down this route.

Pet owner / hobby breeders

Hobby breeders or goat owners will often have great quality kids available. They will tend to have a lot more time for you and will be generally be very attached to the animals they are selling. If you get a goat kid from a local Nubian goat owner who has a spare, then you will also have someone with good knowledge of the breed and a vested interest in the health of your animal, who lives not too far from you.

2. Choosing your goat

If this is your first goat and you're getting them for milk, you should really get a doe with a kid at foot. This means that your goat will be producing milk and you don't have to deal with the breeding or the kidding or any of that scary stuff. It also means that your goat won't be alone, as they need company. In addition, you won't have any of the problems of introducing unfamiliar animals to each other.

Chapter 4 Caring for your goat

1. Housing and pasture

Goats are hardy animals, but they do need a dry, draft-free place to sleep and to escape from the hot sun or rain, and an outdoor space to exercise. If you get a few goats, it's probably worth having a field shelter as well as a shed.

My neighbour keeps pygmies in this goat shed next to his house. Note the kidding shed next to it in the same fenced off area. The ground around the shed is tarmac, meaning that less mud and mess is brought in from outside in the fields.

One important thing to think about when considering your shed is that although your goat doesn't need a lot of height, cleaning out will be a lot easier if you can stand up in the shed. Having something full height will make your life a lot easier. It's also a good idea to have the shed fenced off from the grazing, as you can muck out in winter without having to find them again, and you can keep them somewhere while waiting for vets etc but they won't feel trapped indoors.

In hot areas where protection from sun is important, a simple roof or lean-to might suffice. In a colder climate, you'll need to protect your animal from the cold, the wind, the driving rain and all of the other horrid things we have to contend with. Here a shed is a must, and your goat will need to be able to get out of the weather when they are in the field too.

Most goat raisers recommend anywhere from 12 to 25 square feet of shelter per animal, the lower figure being adequate in warmer climates where they will spend more time outdoors. In cold or wet areas the goats will often be fed indoors and will spend more time there, increasing the space requirement.

Outdoor spaces are equally flexible. You might need little more than a small exercise yard for few goats. Or you might want a pasture area that will provide at least some of the goats' nutritional needs. Lots of people choose to section off the pasture areas so that they can rotate and rest the pasture, getting the most out of your land.

The number of animals you can keep on the land depends on the amount of space you have, the types of plants that grow there, and the food supplements and grain you will be giving. They need to be able to move about freely and to graze on land that is clear of their waste.

Tethering

This is a technique for tying an animal out to graze on a rope. The rope is staked to the ground and the stake can be moved about as the land is grazed. Goats can be tethered with a radius of about 5 metres. If you do tether your goat you need to make sure they always have access to water.

One of the main problems with restricting the movement of your goat is that they must be moved every few hours. It is also now considered quite cruel by a lot of people, as goats are free roaming animals.

There are also some dangers involved in tying up your animal if they are going to have access to enrichments and play as they could become entangled and choke. Tethering isn't really a good long-term solution.

Tethering does have its advantages though. If you need to restrict access to grazing for health reasons, then tethering with a rope is a much simpler and more practical alternative to moving fencing or to having a dedicated, restricted grazing area. It's also good for while you're fixing or replacing fencing, so that your goats can still go out to graze.

Fencing is massively important, though. Goats are notoriously difficult to confine, and they are hard on fencing—especially the cheaper kinds. One good choice for smaller areas is stock panels.

These are made of 1/4″ welded rod and come in 16-ft. lengths, 48 inches high. Other options are limited to such fencing as woven wire, chain link, and electric—the common single-strand type (typically using 2-3 strands), the high-tensile variety, or the netting often referred to as "New Zealand" type fencing. Goats can be trained to respect electric fencing.

One acre of grazing will require 825 feet of fencing—and more if it's not square. Get prices on the kind of fencing you'd like and then add 10% per year for repairs.

2. Food and treats

Goats are ruminants. The term refers to the rumen, the large first compartment of the four-part stomach in which cellulose, mostly from forage, is broken down by organisms living there. This is the basis of feeding goats.

The key to the long-term health of your goat is keeping their diet varied. A varied diet that regularly changes and has new things in will help prevent the gut from getting lazy. A lazy gut can get surprised by sudden, unexpected changes and cause a painful and potentially fatal bloat.

Forage is the mainstay of the goat diet. Forage is things like hay, pasture plants, and browse from trees and bushes. Goats have a reputation for eating everything but they will usually only eat things that are good for them. They may seem odd, as they eat sticks and bark and those tough, woody bits of plants that we wouldn't even attempt. Such coarse materials are indigestible to the goat, but the rumen microbes break them down. You are feeding the microbes, and the microbes feed the goat.

Roughage is essential for goat nutrition. Grains are secondary.

For many people the best, easiest and cheapest way to feed goats is to provide good leafy grass or hay, plus 2-3 pounds a day of a commercial goat feed (grain ration). Others prefer feeding their goats on pasture as much as possible. This can be quite simple, or it can become management-intensive, with controlled rotational grazing, pasture maintenance and renovation, expensive fencing and predator control, to name a few concerns.

Goats also need hay and goat feed to top up their diet and to keep them fed through the winter. A good quality hay can be a real boost for your milk production too.

Most goat feeds available are high in vitamin e and selenium; this helps to avoid various illnesses. They will also be designed for dairy animals, with good levels of everything needed to keep the milk production high and the quality good.

Does who are in milk will need grain. Males will just get fat on too much grain and are greedy little things, so be careful when feeding a mixed herd.

Lots of goat owners grow their own brassicas for themselves to eat and end up sharing them with their goat. A brassicas is a leafy, above ground, non salad vegetable such as cabbage, cauliflower, sprouts and broccoli. These are great for goats and they love to nibble any leaves that are not yet cooked. Goats are a great way to use up the surplus and recycle leafy veg. Don't give them any cooked leftovers though - they aren't suited to eating cooked food. If you have the time and space you could even grow some just for the goats.

Your goat will also need access to salt licks to add minerals to their diet. In the wild, goats will find natural mineral deposits to lick to supplement their intake.

Goats, like all animals, can be fussy about treats, but finding out what treats your goat likes and letting them have a little bit of a treat regularly can be very useful.

If you ever need to give your goat any medicine, and they aren't suspicious of treat time, your life can be made a lot easier by disguising pills or liquid medicines in their favourite nibble. Knowing what treats to use as a bribe also makes training much easier.

Peanuts

Some goats love peanuts, but they might prefer salted, unsalted or still in the shell. If you are giving them salted peanuts, you should restrict access to any salt licks or other dietary salt. Peanuts in their shells also add some good roughage to their diet.

Calf manna

Calf manna is a commercially available treat made from anise, high quality protein, linseed oil, yeast and carbs and is a great source of protein, carbohydrates and vitamins and minerals. Most goats really enjoy calf manna and will gobble it down, eating from your hand if they can. Don't give more than a couple of handfuls a week though – chubby goats aren't healthy goats!

This is also good for any animals recovering from an illness where they have lost weight, such as anorexia, diarrhoea or other digestive problems. It can be used to bulk up animals that are struggling to put on or maintain weight, but if this is a problem that persists, contact your vet for advice.

Any weight problems can by symptomatic of something more sinister than just not being hungry.

Alfalfa

You can get alfalfa cubes for rabbits that goats really love too, but again, not too many. You can also grow alfalfa in a sprouter on your kitchen window from seed, or in window boxes outside. You can also scatter the seeds onto the ground where the pasture grows.

Christmas tree

Christmas trees are delicious. If you contact Christmas tree farms after Christmas, they will usually give you any that they've already cut down. Goats love Christmas trees. They are not only delicious; they make a great game and good scratching posts.

Chips and crisps

Unsalted chips, crisps and tortillas are also a favourite, as they are nice and crunchy, but don't give too many as they can have too much fat in them.

Apples

Chopped up apples are great too, but as they are quite sweet, not in massive amounts. A couple of slices each will be a great treat and won't make them ill.

Carrots

Carrots, on the other hand, aren't too sweet and goats still love them. Carrots have a good nutritional content and are a good, healthy treat.

A lot of goats are partial to a horse cookie here and there, but these can be very sweet and should not be given too often.

Seeds

Sunflower seeds are a great source of oils and fatty acids and are usually appreciated by goats. They also love getting the pine seeds out of pinecones and the pinecone can be a game in itself!

Breakfast cereals

Breakfast cereals make great treats. Frosted ones have too much sugar for a large regular snack, but as an occasional bribe they're ok.

You need to make sure your goats have access to a constant supply of fresh, clean water.

Chapter 5 Settling in your goat

Goats are incredibly intelligent and have a great deal of emotional reactions and responses to things you'd never imagine. So it is important that you take the time to think about your goats' emotional needs as well as their physical needs before moving them in with you.

You need to have everything ready for the new addition to your household. As they are herd animals, you need to consider the emotional wellbeing of your goat when they come to you. A lot of goats on your first venture into goat ownership is not a good idea. So what do you do? It's probably a good idea to get a doe with a kid at foot, so she won't be lonely. If you already have sheep or a horse then you're sorted. Mixed species herds are fairly common among small holders and can be seen in the wild. For evidence of this, you can turn to youtube. There are lots of videos of goats gambolling about with horses, sheep and even dogs.

1. Bonding

You need spend a lot of time bonding with your goat. Goats, like children and dogs, respond to tones of voice. Always use a soft, soothing tone when you are near your goat. It will relax her.

You should spend time around your goat when you are calm and relaxed to make sure your goat recognises you as being safe. Your goat needs to be able to trust you, you'll be milking her, and that requires trust on both parts. You should make sure your goat knows that you will never let them down. If she has an itch, scratch it for her. Never do big, sudden movements that could spook them.

You should groom your goat as much as possible, stroking them, being around them, and getting them used to the idea that you are a source of possible comfort. Express your feelings for your goat in a way that she always will understand and don't be ambiguous.

Don't pull away if the goat tries to sniff or nibble on you. She is simply returning your affection, and will be confused if you don't accept it. Watch the way goats interact with each other. They nibble each other when they are happy and content. Hold your hand out and let her smell you; if you let your goat get used to your scent, it will also help you bond.

2. Preparing for your goat

There are lots of things you need to do to make your goat feel at home. Bring them home, give them access to food and water and let them acclimatise to their surroundings before trying to interact with them.

If your goat is in milk, make sure you know their routine and milk them when their schedule demands. Then you can adjust their timetable gently to suit yours. You should also know how to milk the goat before she arrives.

It is also a good idea to find out what your goat ate before they came to you and feed them this as they adjust, as sudden changes in diet can make goats quite ill.

3. Shopping list

There are a few things you should have before your goat comes home, both for their long-term comfort and just in case anything happens:

Ivermectin
Grass
Feed, hay,
Milking stool and pale
Antiseptic
Wormer
Toys
Styptic
Vaccines
Antiseptic

Electrolyte compound

4. *Logbook*

As an animal owner and enthusiast for all things ordered, I go on and on about logbooks. A logbook or some sort of general record may well save your goat's life one day. It can make everything easier in the long run too.

For many goat owners a logbook may be a little OTT in the way of being organised, but for many others, it can literally be a lifesaver. By keeping precise records that can be accessed and understood by anyone who might require information about your goat's habits, behaviour, feeding and medications, you will be keeping your goat safe, even if you are not the only one looking after them. It could even mean you might be able to go on holiday one day, though that's doubtful, as livestock takes over your life. It can mean your vet may be able to pinpoint the sources or beginning of any illnesses. This will also be useful if you come to sell your goat later on.

The back pages should be a calendar, with dates not days, where you can mark on the worming, farrier and vaccine dates. If you do these things to a strict routine, then there will be far less problems of overlap or missing them out. This is also very useful if there are two or more people involved in the care of the animal. Keeping a record of any medical intervention is very handy too, and knowing when exactly they are administered can help to identify bad interactions.

The front pages should contain a list of useful phone numbers (vet, farrier, insurance details), any regular medications the animal is taking and their description/passport information. This can be very useful in case there are any problems when someone else is watching your goat, for example when you are on holiday.

The internal pages should be a week or 2 per page with a line about each visit to the goat. You should record feed given, any changes in the movement/gait of the goat, interactions with other animals etc. You should also make a record of any time your goat is in transit and how they react to this. If they are ever weighed or measured, you should write this down. If they don't seem to have been eating or drinking, this should also be noted.

Chapter 6 Milking your goat

This is going to be said over and over again – keeping everything clean is vital. Wash everything. If you can't remember whether or not you've done it, wash it again. You'll need a few things, other than a goat, in order to milk your goat.

A stand
Food or treats to keep them occupied if they fret
A stool
A pale
Some udder washing solution

Nubians produce the creamiest milk with very high buttermilk content and lots of protein. Because of this, most Nubian owners choose their goats as dairy animals. If your goat is for milking, you need to know how to milk the animal and be able to milk them regularly. They need milking every 12 hours and it is cruel to milk them less often than this, as it can be very uncomfortable.

Some people think that they don't like the taste of goats' milk and that it has a "goaty" taste. This is only ever because of bacteria fouling the milk, which can almost always be avoided by cleaning your hands and the udder thoroughly. The whole milking area should be scrupulously clean and free from any potential contaminants. There should be no males allowed near the milking area, as they smell and the milk will absorb the smell.

A lot of goat owners do their milking in a separate space where the goats would not be at all in their normal daily routine. This is not only great for keeping the milk free from contaminants, but it's good for training your goat. If she knows that when she goes to a certain place she is going to be milked, she will learn that when she is there she should prepare to be milked, by getting on the stand or positioning herself to be milked.

Lots of goats for which this is true will wait by the gate to the milking area when their udders are feeling uncomfortable. This has many advantages and lets owners know when the animal needs to be milked. This improves the relationship between the owner and the goat as well as the quality and quantity of milk produced, especially if it increases the regularity at which you milk your goat.

Wash the udder and teats with warm water and an udder washing solution (available from farm stores and online), and dry thoroughly. This promotes clean milk but just as importantly stimulates milk "let-down."

Once you're in the swing of it, milking gets easy and becomes a simple part of your daily routine with your animal. It should eventually be a calming time when you both feel safe and close.

First of all, warm up your hands. No one likes a cold shock. Then, take the teat in your hand. Close off the top of the teat with your thumb and forefinger so the milk in the teat will be forced out of the teat, not back into the udder.

Next close your second finger, then the third, and finally your pinkie, forcing the milk out of the teat. Use steady pressure in a rolling motion without pinching or squeezing the teat at all. You can practice this action by placing your fingers on the palm of your hand and pushing down gently with each finger in turn. This way you can feel that you are making an even, rolling pressure.

Discard the first stream from each teat, as it will be high in bacteria, will taste goaty and can foul up the whole batch. This is often the cause of the unpleasant taste people associate with goat's milk. If you always remember to keep this out of the milk you keep then you end up with a much nicer end product for yourself. You do need to make sure you completely strip out the udders to encourage milk production to stay high.

Milk should be weighed and recorded. Weight is used rather than volume because the numbers are easier to work with but also to eliminate guesswork caused by foam.

Strain the warm milk using an approved filter, and cool it immediately and thoroughly. Milk should be chilled to 38° within one hour. The best way to achieve this is by placing the milk container in a pan of ice water for 15-20 minutes, stirring occasionally. Then it can be refrigerated.

Chapter 7 Using goats' milk

There are so many useful things you can do with goat's milk, and as your goat could produce as much as 2-3 litres a day you might need to find an alternative use for the milk.

The people who know and love you will all be aware you have a goat, and may well be a little jealous, and why wouldn't they be? So making things from your milk to give to people is not only a cheep alternative to Christmas presents, but will also be a thoughtful and meaningful gift.

As a lot of people who are lactose intolerant can have goats milk products, you can imagine how much joy you could give to lactose intolerant friends and family members with delicious produce that they can actually enjoy without the worry of health repercussions.

You can do all sorts of things with goats' milk. Goats' milk cheese is delicious and healthier than cow's milk cheese. The butter is also very tasty and making it can really help you keep fit/burn off the excess calories you take in from the butter itself. If all that bashing about isn't to your taste, then goats' milk yoghurt is great pouring yoghurt for breakfast and adding to smoothies. Oh and the ice cream! As an ice cream enthusiast it is difficult to contain yourself when talking about goats' milk ice cream. There are a lot of other foods that goats' milk is a great base for, including some rather good soups. You can also make a great, hearty bread using goats milk. There is also a tasty drink called Kefir that is strange yet delicious and can be made form goat's milk.

Last but not least the soaps and lotions that you can make from goats' milk are said to have all sorts of healthy properties for your skin, as well as making a fabulous gift. Goat's milk is high in vitamins and minerals, in particular vitamin A, which aids in repairing damaged skin. It is also naturally rich in caprylic acid, which soothes and rejuvenates skin.

Goat's milk has fantastic moisturising properties and contains something called alpha hydroxy acid, which a lot of cosmetic companies say reduces the appearance of wrinkles, removes dead skin cells and is generally tip top for your skin. And if you have goats, you don't have to pay anyone extortionate amounts of money for something that may or may not work.

Kefir

Most people have never heard of kefir. Kefir is like a thin drinking yoghurt. There are reams of medical studies with positive results using kefir. They have been conducted for conditions that include diabetes, high cholesterol levels, high blood pressure and many more. It is also a good pro-biotic and is good for recovering from or preventing any gut problems.

If you like kefir, you can use the grains to make it from other things, different types of milk, sugar water, soya or rice milk or even fruit juice.

It is very simple to make and doesn't take very long at all. You just need milk and kefir grains. They look like squishy little cauliflowers and you can buy them online.

Just place the milk kefir grains in milk, give it a quick stir with a non-metal spoon, cover loosely (a towel works great), and allow the kefir to culture on the side for 12 to 24 hours.

After 12 hours, check the kefir every few hours (if possible) so you can remove the kefir grains once the mixture reaches the desired consistency. If your home is on the cool side, it can take a few hours longer for the milk kefir to culture.

Keep the grains as instructed on the packaging and you'll never need to buy any more ever again!

Cheese

There are a number of cheeses you can make with goats milk, from lovely, creamy soft cheeses like Chevre to sliceable, hard cheeses that can be cut into chunks and served on sticks, if that is the sort of thing you do.

Whatever sort of cheese you're making, they all start off the same way – with milk.

You don't need to pasteurise the milk, but some bacteria can really mess up your cheese and make it at best unpalatable. So you need to heat-treat the milk to stop the germs fouling up your cheese.

Heat the milk on the stove, stirring to stop it burning and when it reaches 65C, hold it there for a few minutes. Then allow it to cool to room temperature.

Then just add a cheese culture. You can buy a cheese culture online for very little, and they usually come freeze fried. Follow the instructions on the package and stir up thoroughly. Then leave it for half an hour or so.

Then you add rennet to the mix and stir from the bottom up, for about a minute, before leaving it to settle for 12-24 hours. By this time there will be a thin layer of whey on top of the curd that you can pour off.

From this basic beginning you can make all sorts of cheeses.

For soft cheese (Boursin type), tie the curd in a cheesecloth and hang for a day to drain. Then salt to taste and add herbs, pepper and garlic.

Or, (Chevre type) drain the curds in a mould with holes poked in. Plastic cups are good for this, as you can poke holes in them quite easily. After 2 days, take out of the mould and salt the sides.

Line a cheese mould (of a can of some sort with holes in it) with cheesecloth and scoop the curds into it. Once the curds have settled (half an hour or so) add more curds to the top.

Then you need to put in something called a follower. This is something smaller than the mould that you can put the weights on as you weigh down the cheese as it develops. After 2 days you can remove the cheese from the mould and store in the fridge until it's ready.

If you want to make an aged cheese, or give it as a gift, you can dip the hard cheese in cheese wax and it will be storable for up to 6 months.

For other types of cheese, or more detailed instructions, there are some fantastic books and websites. A quick Internet search will come up with loads of great recipes. You can make Feta types, fruity types and cream cheese types.

Yoghurt

Goat's milk yoghurt is a lot thinner than cow's milk yoghurt, and is like most Greek yoghurt – that's what Greek yoghurt is!

With a litre and a half of milk and 60mls of live yoghurt – preferably goats milk yoghurt- you can make your own very easily.

In a sturdy saucepan, bring your milk to a gentle boil over a medium heat, stirring often; simmer, stirring constantly, for 2 minutes. Pour into a large glass bowl and let it cool until you can hold your finger in the milk for 10 seconds. This will be after about 15 minutes of cooling; don't stick your finger in boiling milk- it will burn you.

In a smaller bowl, whisk together yoghurt and 2 tbsp (30 ml) of the warm milk until it's blended together nicely. Then stir that into remaining the warm milk. Cover it with plastic wrap, then a tea towel and let it stand in a draft-free place until thickened, for about 12 hours. Cover and refrigerate until cold.

You can keep this in the fridge for up to a week and it goes nicely with fruit, cereal and ice cream.

Ice cream

Because goat's milk generally has less water, more fat, less lactose and more solids than cow's milk, it makes a thick, creamy delicious ice cream with a very good flavour.

A basic vanilla ice cream can be made like this:
2 cups goat milk
½ vanilla bean or 1 tablespoon of vanilla extract
4 egg yolks
⅓ cup honey
1 tablespoon of cornstarch

Mix together the egg yolks, ½ cup of goat's milk and the cornstarch until smooth in a blender.

If using a vanilla bean, split it and scrape out the seeds. Add the pod and seeds to the goat's milk in the next step. If using vanilla extract, it will be added in at the end of the cooking process.

Add the remaining goat's milk and honey to a heavy bottomed, medium saucepan (preferably one with a pouring lip), and bring to a rolling boil on a medium heat. Boil, stirring for 3 minutes.

Remove the saucepan from the burner. Turn the blender on at a low setting and in a very, very thin stream and pour in the hot goat's milk. It is critical that this is done very slowly so as not to end up with scrambled eggs. Do this through the access hole in your blender lid as opposed to just having the lid off, otherwise you risk making a surprising and regrettable mess.

When the goat's milk mix is fully incorporated with the eggs, turn off the blender and pour the mix back into the pan you used to heat the goat's milk.

Thicken the mixture into an egg custard by stirring constantly, over a medium heat, until you measure 170° F/77° C on a good instant read thermometer. If you don't have an instant read thermometer, thicken it until you can run your finger over the back of the spoon or spatula you are stirring with and leave a trail that doesn't immediately fill back in.

Remove from the heat. Remove the two pieces of vanilla bean pod. If using vanilla extract instead, mix it in now.

Pre-chill the mixture before freezing it in your ice cream maker.

Freeze the mixture in your ice cream maker. It should take 15 – 30 minutes.

Serve right out of your maker or within a few hours of storing in your freezer. Store the remainder in a freezer proof container. A layer of cling film smoothed on to the top of the ice cream before you close the container will help keep air out and frost from forming.

You can add other flavours to this and leave out the vanilla. For example, ginger syrup and crystallised ginger make a great, zingy ice cream that really impresses.

Or you can do a chocolate chunk ice cream with cocoa and sugar in the mix and throwing in some high quality chocolate pieces at the end.

Or in the summer you can add fresh hedgerow fruit, like raspberries or blackberries, to make a refreshing ripple of flavour.

Bread

Bread made with goat's milk is a delicious, hearty addition to the table. The fat in the milk makes for a great texture in the bread, and it keeps for up to 3 days as long as you don't put it in the fridge - the cold, dry air in the fridge crystallises the bread, making it go stale quicker.

250g strong white bread flour
1 tsp fast-action dried yeast
1 tbsp olive oil
200ml goat's milk
Salt

Mix together the flour, yeast and 1/2 tsp salt. Add the oil, and then pour in the water gradually, adding enough to make soft dough. Knead the dough on a lightly floured surface for about 4-5 minutes until the dough feels strong, and stretchy. The key to good bread is elasticity.

Put on a floured baking tray in a warm place while the dough rises or proves. Once it's doubled in size, knock the air out to redistribute the bubbles, give it a **quick** knead and leave to rise again. Then bake the bread in a preheated oven at 210C oven for 45 minutes or until the crust is crunchy. Then serve warm with hot soup.

Soup

Most vegetable soups can be truly complimented with goats' milk. In the winter, a nice, filling squash or carrot soup that is thick and creamy can really warm up the day.

This recipe is for squash, but you can substitute carrots, parsnips or any other winter vegetable, or use a mixture depending on what you have.

1 large squash – diced or sliced
6 tsp olive oil
6 cloves of peeled and crushed garlic, or a good dollop of the stuff from a tube
1 medium onion - diced
1 tsp pepper
2 pints of goat's milk
Pinch of salt.

Roast the squash (or whatever vegetable you're using) in a preheated oven at 170C for 30 minutes. Then add the garlic, olive oil and onion, mix everything up and return to the oven for another half an hour.

Put a quarter of the milk in a blender with the squash and everything else that's been roasted and wiz it up into a fine puree. Then put this in a pan and heat up. As it is heating, add more milk.

Do not allow to boil.

When the soup is hot enough, add the pepper to taste and serve with crusty bread and a dollop of butter.

Butter

You need a pint of goat cream to make butter. This means that you need to separate the cream from a few days worth of milking. To do this, you have to make sure the milk sits undisturbed in the fridge for a day, then take the cream off, and use the rest of the milk in your tea or for breakfast or whatever you normally do, and repeat this with another few days of milk.

Then you need to chill some beaters, water and a bowl in the fridge. These need to be properly cold by the time you use them. Then, heat up the cream using the temperature of the room until it's a little over 50F. The contrast in temperature here makes the process much easier.

Then whip up the cream until it's whipped like you'd put on a cake. Then keep going. Keep going until the cream begins to split. Keep going past the point where you'd have done it wrong if you were making whipped cream and then keep going some more. Little globules of butter will be forming, surrounded by a thin, white liquid. As soon as the globules start to cluster together, stop whipping. You're done with that bit.

Next you just strain the butter, gently, in cheesecloth to let out the remaining liquid. You can use this in lotions or mix it in with pig feed.

Then turn the butter out into a dish or onto cling film and shape it and put it into the fridge.

Soap

If you're doing soap, you need to be very careful of some of the chemicals used. GOGGLES AND GLOVES are an absolute must, as you don't want your hands and eyes turning into soap. Seriously. That can happen so be careful.

26.5 oz. Olive oil

20 oz. Frozen goat's milk (freeze in ice cube tray)
16.5 oz Coconut oil
10 oz. Vegetable oil, preferably Rape Seed and not Palm Oil
209 grams Lye

You should use frozen goat's milk, as the Lye causes a chemical reaction with the liquid and gets very hot. Burning the milk and messes everything up, so using it frozen really helps. You should also keep the mixture in a bowl that is inside another bowl of ice water.

Melt all the oils and fats together and leave to stand, but do not leave to set.

With your goggles and gloves on, pour the lye into the goat milk ice/slush and stir constantly. Add the lye as slowly as you can and try to keep the mixture cool.

Check the temperature of both of your mixtures, and when they are both around 115F, you can combine them, stirring gently as you go, keeping your gloves and goggles on.

Using a stick blender, blend the mixture until it has reached an even consistency, with no globules of fat visible. If you want, you should add any essential oils or herbs at this point rather than later.

Pour into the receptacles of your choice and leave for at least 4 weeks. If you want to, you can cut it up after 24 hours into bars, but DO NOT TOUCH WITH SKIN FOR AT LEAST 4 WEEKS as soap burn, though it might seem ridiculous, is a real thing and can do you some very unpleasant damage.

Lotion

Homemade lotions are fun and easy to make. They are a great alternative for those with sensitive skin. Read any label on generic skin care and you will know how hard it is to find a product without a long list of ingredients. As a goat owner you will have access to a large amount of good quality goat's milk that you can use as and when you have a surplus.

1 cup goat's milk

1/8 cup pure olive oil

1/8 tsp white vinegar (*acts as a natural preservative*)

Simply whisk the milk and oil together until it has formed a thick, creamy consistency. If you've ever made your own mayonnaise, you'll know that this can take a very long time, but once it's done you'll have a lovely consistency. Then mix in the vinegar to stop it going off.

You can add scented oils to add a little variety, but make sure that they're skin safe and that you're not sensitive to them. In an airtight jar you can keep these lotions at room temperature for quite a long time, and if they separate out, simply re-mix them up again until they're back at a good texture.

Chapter 8 Health

Goats are hardy and generally healthy animals. With proper nutrition and management, illness is rare. But of course, any living creature can get sick.

The health of your goats, as with any animals in your care, is not only a moral responsibility, but also a legal one. In the UK and the USA you can be prosecuted for having an untreated, sick animal.

The way to avoid this is to keep an eye on the health of your animal, to keep up to date on vaccinations, and, importantly, to know what to look out for.

Pica

Pica is a psychological illness that makes animals crave non-food items. Goats aren't really prone to pica in the way that some people and dogs can develop it, but they do eat things that aren't food. This isn't an illness, per say, but it can cause some horrid problems.

As goats are bright and inquisitive, and as, like human children, they explore much of their world by putting things in their mouth, they can end up getting themselves into more trouble than other agricultural animals. You have to keep a real eye out for anything they can reach that can make them ill.

This includes non-digestible, non-food items, such as plastic and clothing. This can clog up in the gut causing swelling and constipation. If enough rotting faecal matter backs up in any animal, it can be fatal.

Usually, goats don't eat non-food items unless they are starving, but they will often chew things up to see what happens and they can accidentally swallow things.

Obviously, you can't watch your goat all the time and there may be instances of a plastic grocery bag blowing into the pasture and being gobbled up without you noticing. What happens next, in these situations, can be the difference between life and death. Small amounts of plastic may be ground up in the stomach and passed with little or no consequence, but spotting the signs of a clog early means that your goat can be treated quickly.

If you suspect the goat has eaten something they shouldn't have, start watching out for excretions and any unusual behaviour, such as an achy stomach, irritableness, fever. I think I would give them mineral oil orally. Be careful though as they cannot taste mineral oil & they can aspirate it very easily.

If you follow this then you should never be in a position where a goat gets a big blockage of non-digestible gubbins in their gut. If this does happen you will be able to feel that the abdomen is harder than usual. Your goat will become very irritable and it's appetite will diminish.

1. Vaccinations

There are so many illnesses that can damage the health of your goat that you need to do everything you can to avoid them. The easiest way to do that is to vaccinate. The four most common vaccinations for goats are tetanus, white muscle disease, Enterotoxaemia and Enterotoxaemia.

Tetanus

Tetanus is a horrific illness, causing stiffness in joints, muscle rigidity, hyperesthesia and convulsions, often followed by a slow, painful death. It comes from microbes in soil, wood or metal that get into the blood through cuts and scrapes.

You can avoid this whole thing with a simple vaccination, recommended for all livestock.

White-muscle disease

White-muscle disease is a degenerative illness that can be found in all large animals and is caused by a deficiency in selenium and/or vitamin E. As the name suggests, it affects the muscles, both skeletal and cardiac.

Symptoms that the skeletal muscles are affected by are a real pain in walking and the muscles become stiff. The gait will be abnormal and the back may be arched. They'll become weak and listless.

Symptoms that the animal's cardiac muscles have been affected are like symptoms of pneumonia. There will be difficulty breathing, snot and a fever. The heart rate will be irregular and fast, as will the breathing.

Treatments for white-muscle disease is not always affective, and animals who've had cardiac problems will rarely survive, and if they do, they certainly won't do well. Vaccinations are available though, and your vet will be able do advise you on them.

Enterotoxaemia

Enterotoxaemia, or overeating disease, is a very unpleasant illness that affects goats of all ages. It is caused by bacteria in the gut that overpopulates the gut, making the animal lethargic and causing stomach pain and diarrhoea.

The animal could stop being able to walk or stand. By the time the goat is struggling to stand it is too late and the poor thing will probably be dead in less than an hour. There is no real guaranteed treatment for this illness.

You can avoid this by good management and vaccinations. Your vet will be able to advise you about this.

Pasteurellosis

Pasteurellosis is an infectious disease infecting the blood and the lungs. It is a pneumonia like illness that can kill your goat.

Symptoms include a vague depression and anorexia. There will be a little weight loss and listlessness. Breathing will then become difficult and weight loss with increase. The animal may cough and develop a snotty nose.

The prognosis for animals with pasteurellosis isn't good. In the later stages it doesn't respond well to antibiotics and the animal will probably die.

You can avoid this by good management and vaccinations. Your vet will be able to advise you about this.

Remember, vaccines are not cures: they're preventatives. You need to vaccinate before any illness is present and vaccinate regularly. This is where your logbook will come in handy.

2. Illnesses and health problems

Abortion

Abortions in goats will mostly occur from 6-8 weeks of pregnancy, and veterinary treatment is needed immediately to prevent infertility. You also need to make sure that the foetus is delivered as soon as possible so that it doesn't release toxins that will kill the mother too. Abortion could occur due to drinking water containing *salmonella typhinmurium*. Abortion can occur in a goat fed on rich clover or trefoil too.

Acetonemia

Acetonemia, also called Ketosis Toxemia is another horrid problem in goats – mainly pregnant does, caused by a lack of carbs in the diet.

Symptoms include: loss of appetite, swelling legs, sluggishness and staggering/appearing drunk. If treated at this point, there should be no development of the other symptoms, such as blindness, ataxia and coma. If the doe does fall into a coma, the foetuses will die inside the mother, releasing potentially fatal toxins into her.

At the first sign of any of these symptoms, add a high-energy supplement to the doe's diet, up the carbohydrate intake and start feeding "goat magic". Goat Magic is made from 1 part molasses, 2 parts Kayro Syrup, and 1 part corn oil. You can adjust the amounts as needed as long as you keep the proportions the same. Lots of goat owners keep a jar of this ready made in case anything happens to their animals. Because it is made from all shed or housing ingredients, it will last for ages as long as you keep it in a sealed container.

A good rule of thumb for avoiding this is to up the carbohydrate content of the diet when a goat is pregnant. The more kids you think she's carrying, the more carbohydrates she needs. You might even consider a spoon of goat magic in the daily feed.

If you're ever worried about your goat, even if you suspect you know what's wrong and you know how to treat it or not, you should seek veterinary advice.

Lice, fleas, mites and parasites

While many goats do not seem to get fleas, there are some that are affected and you should keep an eye on your animals. If they do get fleas, they can be treated with capstar tablets or spot on. If using capstar to treat fleas, any milk should be discarded for 3 days after treatment. Capstar works by poisoning the fleas and the effects on the milk are not positive. Do not stop milking the goat, as she will dry off. Goats can also get mites, lice and worms.

A heavy parasite burden can cause serious anaemia and with goats this can be fatal much quicker than with larger animals. Even if your goat survives a serious parasite burden, they could be left with some pretty horrific health problems as a result of organ damage. This is easily avoided, however, with the correct, regular preventative treatment and observation.

Mites, lice, ticks and other external parasites can be kept in check with regular grooming.

Goats need worming every 8 weeks. You can do this yourself with an oral de-wormer such as Ivermectin. If your goat is very young or stressed you should use a milder wormer or a daily wormer.

Diarrhoea

This can be caused by a number of things including infections in the upper or lower gut and eating inappropriate foods or even a change in diet. Diarrhoea, whatever the underlying cause, can be fatal and any goat with diarrhoea should be given plenty of water with electrolytes. It causes rapid dehydration and you seek veterinary advice as soon as you notice any faeces that are loose or watery. Diarrhoea can kill much quicker than you might expect, as the salts and water lost are difficult to replace once the damage has begun.

If your goat has diarrhoea, you need to keep their bedding scrupulously clean and be very aware of hygiene, as if an infection has caused the problem, the animal could accidentally re-infect itself.

Affected animals should be kept away from other animals to avoid further contamination. Your emergency kit should contain ProBalance or some pro-biotic and, oddly enough, liquorice. The pro-biotic should help to restore the lost gut flora and the liquorice should reduce digestive inflammation. You still need to see your vet about underlying causes. Seek veterinary advice.

Arthritis

Arthritis is a painful, progressive and limiting illness that affects many of us. It can also affect goats. The symptoms are fairly obvious and are shown as decreased range of movement or less willingness to move about as much.

There are treatments that can alleviate the pain, though there is not yet a cure. If your goat develops arthritis, your vet will go through the various treatment options, and you should not consider arthritis the end of the animal's healthy life – they can still continue to have a good quality of life. The long-term prognosis for goats is better than that of larger animals. Because there is less weight on the joints and less pressure on the feet, they tend to suffer less if they do contract arthritis than other, larger livestock, such as cattle and horses. This is a condition that can be managed in a way that doesn't affect the milk. Seek veterinary advice.

Anaemia

Anaemia is often a symptom of other problems and can be shown by a general paleness. The lips, guns and udder will be paler than usual and the goat may become lethargic. Anaemia is simply a lack of iron in the goat, starving the cells of oxygen. It can be low iron in the blood, or low blood in the goat. Treatment can be done by the use of iron injection 5ml Dexavin (Pfizer) or Ferrofax (Duphar). Seek veterinary advice.

Rinderpest

Rinderpest is an acute, highly contagious diseasecaused by a Morbillivirus. In its acute form it is characterised by inflammation and necrosis of mucous membranes and a very high mortality rate. It is normally found in cattle, but has been known to cross into sheep and goats.

I you have an infected animal you need to contact the authorities. In the UK that's DEFRA and in the USA it's the department of agriculture.

Symptoms include mild thermal reaction and diarrhoea. Ulcerative lesions appear inside the lower tip and gums. Luckily, rinderpest is mostly found in Africa and is on the decline. If you do encounter an instance of this horrific illness, your animal will be destroyed and the carcass will need to be disposed of properly. Seek veterinary advice.

Anorexia

Though normally associated with young humans, anorexia can occur in any animal. The most important thing to find out is the cause. A loss of appetite could be voluntary Anorexia or Pathological Anorexia.

Symptoms include loss of appetite and weight loss. A milker will produce less milk and loose weight very rapidly. If there is a kid at foot, the kid may be adversely affected by this too.

Contact the vet for advice and feed your animal up. Calf manna is a great way to help your goat put on weight quickly.

Anthrax

That's right- anthrax. Anthrax is an acute disease caused by the bacterium *Bacillus anthracis,* which can survive all sorts of conditions and remain dormant in the ground until they find themselves in a host, where they will multiply and make animals horrifically ill.

Symptoms include sudden high temperatures (108°F), loss of appetite, sudden death and in less acute forms goat may live for a day and develop bloody diarrhoea.

You can avoid anthrax by keeping an eye on other animals that come into contact with yours and making sure that they are healthy. If you show or regularly move your goat, you should keep a record of where and when they have moved in the logbook. Keep the affected animal separate. Annual vaccination of goats in endemic area is recommended.

If you suspect anthrax, you need to contact DEFRA or the Department of Agriculture. It is a notifiable disease and the consequences for not notifying the authorities are severe. In fact, any sudden, unexplained deaths in your goat should be reported. There have been no cases of anthrax in the UK since 2006, but it can lay dormant in the ground and become a problem later. Anthrax spores remain viable for decades in the soil or on animal products such as dried or processed hides or wool. Spores can survive for two years in water, 10 years in milk and up to 71 years on silk threads. You should check to make sure the land you're using has never had any cases.

Bronchitis

This occurs due to lungworm infection or other infections causing damage to the lung.

Symptoms include coughing and listlessness.

Brucellosis

This is a horrid illness caused by *Brucella organisms.*

Symptoms include abortion in late pregnancy where retention of placenta and metritis are common. In male goats it causes infertility, orchitis and swollen joints are seen.

Goats should be tested for brucellosis and you have to isolate or cull the positive animals.

Seek veterinary advice.

Big-Head

This is an acute, infectious disease, caused by bacteria. The disease is characterized by a rapid and unsightly swelling of the head, face, and neck, most commonly seen in young rams and bucks. This infection is initiated in young rams and bucks by their continual butting of one another. The bruised and battered subcutaneous tissues provide conditions suitable for growth of the bacteria, and the breaks in the skin offer an opportunity for their entrance.

Treatment may be possible with broad-spectrum antibiotics or penicillin if the disease is caught early. The disease may be prevented by vaccination against the bacteria involved.

Vaccinate pregnant ewes and does with 7-way or 8-way vaccine during the last 30 days of pregnancy. The resulting high levels of antibodies in the colostrums should protect the lambs/kids. Vaccinate lambs/kids with a 7-way or 8-way vaccine at 30 days of age, and follow up with a booster in 2 to 4 weeks.

Vaccination may be necessary every 6 months, though this could be less if you have better mannered animals or you don't have intact males living together. Seek veterinary advice about this one.

Bloat

Bloat is caused by a number of things, and can be a serious condition that, if left untreated, can result in death to the goat. A build up of gas in the stomach and intestines caused by a rumen imbalance causes swelling, discomfort and occasionally ruptures.

It can be caused by overeating and consuming too much fibre. It can be caused by too much pasture and weeds – they are quite good at only eating things that are good for them, but as they are greedy, they sometimes eat weeds that can upset their tummies. A sudden change in diet can also cause bloat, especially if their regular diet doesn't have much variation in it.

Symptoms include a distended (stretched out) abdomen, especially on the left side, an inability or unwillingness to move about and lying down a lot.

Treatment depends on the cause, which you can usually determine from looking back over your logbook. Have they gotten into the feed bins lately? Then it'll be an overeating problem. Has your goat been left out in a new pasture area or broken into a neighbour's garden? Then it's probably weeds. Has your grain supplier changed? Then the problem is probably caused by the diet change.

After working out what's caused the bloat, call a vet and if the goat can walk, walk them up and down a bit. Then give about a quarter of a pint of cooking oil and massage their sides. If the goat can release the gas on its own it will be a lot less invasive, so help it to move about and stretch. Wait for the vet. A little bicarbonate of soda and molasses is good for helping to relieve the bloat while you're waiting.

If the bloat is caused by weeds and the goat is likely to get out into the weeds again, leave a pan of bicarbonate of soda and molasses in some water with the goat to prevent it reoccurring.

You can prevent a change of diet by always feeding the animal a good variety so that the digestion doesn't get lazy.

Cheesy Gland (CL)

This is a horrid illness that is also called yolk boils (Caseous lymphadenitis). This painful disease is caused by the bacterium coryne and bacterium pseudo tuberculosis. It causes abscesses and boils that can be seen as swollen lumps under the jaw or on the neck. In goats, the head is most commonly affected, so the most likely point of entry of this infection is through cuts and scrapes on the head or in the mouth.

To avoid this illness, five different brands of cheesy-gland vaccines are available: Glanvac, cheesyvax, cydectin, Eweguard, Guardian and Websters 6-in-1.

To treat this illness, in goats with large abscesses, lance the abscess at the lowest point. Flush out the cavity with disinfectant after the pus has drained. Because pus is the main method of spread, it should be collected and disposed of safely by burying or treating with disinfectant. You should get a vet to show you this.

Obesity

Nubian goats are far more prone to overeating than larger goats, and because of their stature, the relative weight gain is greater. Because of the smaller size of their gut, Nubian goats are only able to process small amounts of food at a time and so should be fed often, but only small amounts. Goats are less likely to get the exercise and restriction of access to pasture. Owners of larger goats can have real emotional niggles about feeding their minis so much less than everyone else. If your goat does become overweight, you need to seek veterinary advice before restricting the diet, as there could be an underlying cause (other than gluttony).

Diarrhoea

This can be caused by a number of things including infections in the upper or lower gut and eating inappropriate foods or even a change in diet. Diarrhoea, whatever the underlying cause, can be fatal and any goat with diarrhoea should be given plenty of water with electrolytes. It causes rapid dehydration and you seek veterinary advice as soon as you notice any faeces that is loose or watery.

If your goat has diarrhoea you need to keep their bedding scrupulously clean and be very aware of hygiene, as if an infection has caused the problem, the animal could accidentally reinfect itself.

Affected animals should be kept away from other animals to avoid further contamination. Your emergency kit should contain

ProBalance or some probiotic and, oddly enough, liquorice. The probiotic should help to restore the lost gut flora and the liquorice should reduce digestive inflammation. You still need to see your vet about underlying causes.

Septicaemia

Septicaemia is a deadly bloodstream infection that can kill an animal very quickly. Septicaemia is the presence of bacteria or bacterial toxins in the bloodstream, and can kill very quickly. As Nubian goats are smaller, they will succumb to the infection even faster than larger goats. The higher risk of death makes this a very serious illness and you need to be constantly on the lookout for septicaemia and seek veterinary advice as soon as you spot any signs, as early detection can literally be the difference between life and death. The younger the animal, the more danger it will be in, due to the weaker immune system. It is also far more likely in foals that have not had their colostrums.

There is no vaccination for this so you need to be very vigilant. It can often be treated with antibiotics, but not always, so prevention is the key. Any cuts, grazes or scrapes need to be treated with antiseptic cream and kept clean. This includes cuts in the mouth and splits in the hoof. Anywhere that any blood or flesh is in contact with the outside world, needs to be kept clean. Unlike a lot of equine aliments, septicaemia isn't contagious by external contact.

Feet

Just like horses and other hoofed animals, goats' hooves need regular trimming. In the wild, these growths are kept under control by constant scrambling over rocks. Left untouched, overgrown hooves can cripple an animal by throwing bones out of alignment.

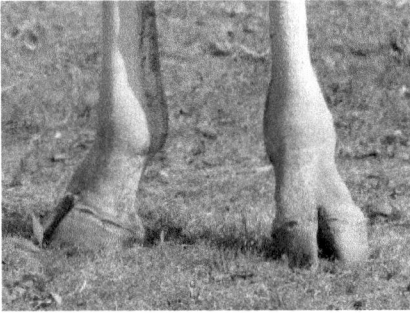

Hoof trimming can be accomplished with a sharp knife (and a great deal of care), but the ideal is a hoof trimmer, shears made for the purpose, available from goat and sheep supply houses. An alternative is ordinary sharp rose pruning shears. Leather gloves are a good idea. Most people will want to have a helper, or a milking stand to help restrain the goat.

Moving the leg back so the hoof faces up, first clean out any muck and dirt. Next trim off any bent-over parts of the hoof. It should be even with the bottom of the foot, but just take a little at a time until you gain experience. The hoof will show pink as you near the blood supply.

The toe, or point of the hoof, wears down less than the sides and requires more trimming. Heels seldom need trimming, but check them just in case.

Regular walking on hard surfaces may wear the hoof down and mean less hoof trimming, but you should keep a watch on the feet anyway.

Eyes

The eyes of a goat are very sensitive. All animals can get infections, disorders, and diseases of the eyes, including goats. Keeping the eyes clear of infections and diseases is important for the overall health of this unique animal. Cancers and tumours of the eyes can occur in goats. Keeping the eyes clean and knowing what your Nubian goat's eyes usually look like is very important and any changes in discharge or any damage should result in you seeking immediate veterinary attention.

Goats, like many animals, can be born with blindness. However, there are several diseases and illnesses that can lead to blindness and should be monitored closely. Poisoning from lead, pesticides, and some plants have lead to blindness. Diseases such as pregnancy toxemia and Vitamin A deficiencies can also cause blindness in goats. It is important to treat the underlying disease or illness before blindness occurs if possible.

Ears

Goat's ears need to be kept clean and clear from any mites and from infection. Any problems with the ear can transfer to problems elsewhere or could be symptomatic of other illnesses. Any unusual discharge from the ear should be checked out.

Horns

The issue with goat's horns is disbudding. It is highly controversial and can get you into all sorts of hotly debated arguments, whichever side you come down on.

Disbudding or de-horning is the removal of the horn buds in goat kids, and/or the removal of horns from adult goats is a procedure that can only be carried out by a veterinary surgeon in the UK. The Royal College of Veterinary Surgeons considers the act of disbudding to be a mutilation, and as such requires serious thought before being undertaken, but it is accepted that for management and welfare reasons it is often necessary in larger goat enterprises.

As the horn bud grows extremely rapidly in goat kids they should be disbudded between 2-7 days old, and must only be done by a vet with the kids under general anaesthesia +/- local nerve blocks.

Lots of people don't like disbudding, because goat kids have very thin skulls and disbudding carried out by an untrained person can easily cause irreparable damage to the brain, either by direct heat transfer damage, or by facilitating the entry of bacteria into the skull, leading to a potentially fatal meningitis.

Many people argue that it's not really needed, especially if you're only going to have a couple of does. Because Nubians grow so big, they are often safer without their horns. If you're having a few living together, having no horns can avoid serious injury.

The main advantage of having no horns is that they cannot grow back, towards the head. Ingrown horns will need major surgery and are unnecessarily painful.

Don't give your goat any medication without consulting your vet as this can cover up symptoms, meaning you could think your goat has recovered. Keeping a logbook record of food and behaviour may make it easier to pinpoint the cause and start of the problem.

3. When to take your goat to the vet

A lot of little niggles and things that might worry your goat will need treating, but not always by a vet. Most scrapes and scratches and a little cold should be treated immediately to avoid infections, but you can usually do this yourself. There are times, however, when veterinary intervention is absolutely vital. There are also times when it's hard to say- they might not *need* to see the vet but it's always better safe than sorry.

A good rule of thumb is; when in doubt, seek veterinary advice. Even if friends or neighbours, or even books have told you that you don't need to see a vet, if you are unsure, phone them. They may reassure you over the phone that it's fine, or they may come out and save the goat's life.

Becoming unresponsive

If for any reason- that you know of or if you can't work out why- your goat becomes unresponsive you must seek veterinary advice as soon as possible. Not responding to noise can suggest ear infections, deafness or head trauma. Ignoring the sight and movement of those around it can suggest any number of illnesses, including infections, problems with eyesight and physical distress.

Thirst or hunger

Excessive thirst or hunger can be a sign of all sorts of horrid things, such as poisoning, diabetes and infections. Don't panic immediately though. The first thing that you need to check is whether or not your goat has had access to enough clean water. If not then that could explain why they are so thirsty. If they have not had access to water for some time you may still want to consult your vet, as dehydration can make animals very poorly. But if there was sufficient water and they drank it all, and continued to be thirsty, this could mean your animal is unwell.

Seek veterinary advice.

Poison

If your goat has ingested something you know or even suspect to be poisonous, or even if you only think they may have, you must seek veterinary advice immediately.

Seizure

If your goat has any sort of seizure, no matter how small, go to the vet. A seizure can look like a small, sudden collapse that seems quickly recovered from or it can be a collapse followed by a worrying time of incapacity and possibly shaking. It can also be very subtle, with all of the muscles tensing up and the goat becoming rigid. Most animals suffering from a seizure will evacuate their bowels. If you suspect a seizure, seek veterinary advice.

Strange movement

If your goat begins to move strangely and you can't see a reason; for example if they aren't used to being tethered, seek veterinary advice. Strange movements can be an indication of neurological problems, or it could be an early indication of narcolepsy. Strange movements can also be associated with physical discomfort. A goat with arthritis, tetanus or any bone or muscle damage will need treating immediately. It could also just be a hoof that needs cleaning better, so make sure you check the possibilities.

Fur loss

Fur loss is often indicative of a lice infestation or poor health and condition. If you are confident that your goat does not have any external parasites, you should seek veterinary advice for both treatment of the fur loss and the underlying cause.

Lumps and bumps

If you feel an abnormal lump, it isn't necessarily cancer, but you need to seek immediate veterinary help, as even a benign fat lump can make your goat uncomfortable or ill. Other lumps may be fluid trapped underneath the skin; this is called dependent edema and could be a sign of arteritis, a very serious illness. Any bruises should be looked at and the cause of any bruising should be investigated and, where possible, removed.

Bleeding

Any profuse bleeding, obviously, needs to be seen by the vet. A little scratch will usually be ok, but even a small cut can become infected and an infection needs to be treated by the vet before septicaemia sets in. You should have an antiseptic rub in your emergency kit. If a small cut takes a long time to heel, you can treat it with styptic. You should also have styptic in your emergency kit.

Broken bones

This is very obvious but any serious injury or wound of any kind needs veterinary help. If you even suspect any broken bones, your goat needs urgent veterinary attention.

Discharge from the eyes or nose

This could be a symptom of a serious repertory illness, or just a little sniffle. It's always better safe than sorry and if your goat does have a repertory infection, the sooner it is treated the better. If any discharge continues for more than a couple of days, is excessive, contains any blood or is coupled with any other symptoms, you should seek veterinary advice.

Don't give your goat any medication without consulting your vet as this can cover up symptoms, meaning you could think your goat has recovered. Keeping a logbook record of food and behaviour may make it easier to pinpoint the cause and start of the problem.

4. Emergency kit

There are a few things you should have on hand with any pet. With most pets you can get the things you'll need in an emergency quite readily at a local store or super market. Goats, however, are not very common pets, and should the occasion arise, there are a few things you should have in case of an emergency. An animal first aid kit is an old idea, but a good one.

Styptic

Styptic is a clotting agent used by used all sorts of people for all sorts of reasons. Men use it when they cut themselves shaving; rabbit owners use it when they cut the claws too short. When sprinkled on small cuts that bleed for too long, styptic is a fantastic clotting aid and can help a wound heel quickly, avoiding infection. It comes in stick form for human use, but is also available as a powder, such as Kwik-Stop Styptic Powder and works out at about $10 or £7 an ounce. Most goat owners won't use anywhere near that in an animals lifetime.

Antiseptic

An antiseptic gel like Radiol B-R antibacterial Jelly or a spray like Purple Spray can help avoid all sorts of problems. Applied directly and immediately to any minor cuts, scrapes and grazes, an anti-bacterial agent can stop infections occurring, potentially saving hundreds, if not thousands in veterinary bills, as well as a lot of pain and distress for your goat. Any infections should be treated immediately by the vet to avoid septicaemia, and any real wounds need to be looked at by a vet anyway.

Electrolyte compound

Keeping a compound of electrolytes handy could well save your goat's life if they ever develop any diarrhoea or dehydration. If there is ever any point at which your goat is ill, they could easily become dehydrated and die of dehydration rather than the initial illness.

Probiotics

Because of the complex nature of goat digestion, it is important that their gut flora is kept healthy. If there has been any problem with digestion, whether it be sudden weight loss or just a small bout of diarrhoea, replacing the 'good' bacteria and promoting its health in the animal's gut is vitally important.

Chapter 9 Play and enrichment

Goats are intelligent animals and are easily bored. A bored animal is an unhappy animal, and as an owner it is your responsibility to keep your goat happy. You can't be with them all of the time, but you can and should provide entertainment.

Most fields don't have mountains or cliffs for goats to exercise their natural behaviours, so you need to provide some way for them to do that.

Even a pile of logs or a little wall will be appreciated.

There is a wide range of toys available to keep goats occupied. A lot of these toys will involve a food treat. You can use this as an opportunity to give your goat some much needed dietary supplements. You can get toy compatible treats that contain all sorts of things, from salt licks to cod-liver oil. Many owners also use these treat toys to administer wormer and other medications.

1. Bought toys

There are lots of websites that sell boredom busters for goats. These clever companies make all sorts of food based enrichment toys that can keep your goat entertained when you're not around.

Hanging likit holder

There are all sorts of hanging holders for salt licks and treats out there. They are a fantastic way to keep your goat entertained and healthy, as you can use them to introduce electrolytes, vitamins and other dietary supplements. These devices hang from the ceiling and contain delicious things that are good for your goat and that they want to lick at. Because it is hanging, it moves around and the goat will have to move their head and neck about to taste and bite their treat. This provides a nice bit of mental exercise.

Tongue twister

The tongue twister is a similar thing to the hanging holder, but it can be attached to the shed or housing wall or to fence posts and trees. It holds the treat and the goat has to twist their tongue around to get at it. The device doesn't move about but its components do, moving and getting in the way of the enquiring tongue and making the goat think and move about.

Boredom Breaker

This is a clever hanging toy with a hanging lickit holder and a ball suspended from the bottom of the string. The ball has a compartment for more treats and because the ball turns around, the treats aren't always at the front for the goat to access, so the goat has to use their mind a bit to get at their treat.

Treat balls

The Snak-a-ball (http://www.likit.co.uk/) or Pasture Pal
(http://www.equi-spirit-toys.com) or Nose-It (http://www.nose-
it.com) are very similar to treat balls for smaller animals and can
be filled with whatever feed you use for your goat. It rolls around
on the ground and the goat nudges it to move it about. The food
falls out of the hole in small amounts for the goat to eat. This is
excellent because not only does it keep your goat occupied, it also
keeps the food relatively clean while encouraging natural grazing
behaviours, which have a beneficial effect on the mental
wellbeing of animals in captivity.

Balls

There is a whole range of balls for goats to play with, from
traditional footballs (soccer balls) to balls with handles that they
can carry about with them. The amazing thing is that goats will
play with these with very little encouragement, and if left alone
with them, will play with them whenever they want.

2. *Homemade toys and how to make them*

Things with the word "goat" in front of them will often come
with a high price tag, but that doesn't mean you can't keep your
goat entertained without breaking the bank. There are all sorts of
toys you can make yourself or adapt from other things.

Ice-lolly

On very hot days, your goat needs to keep cool. A good way to
help them do this is to chop up some of their favourite fruits and

veggies and freeze then in a block of water. Old ice cream or margarine tubs make good ice trays and make ice-lollies of about the right size. Ice should only be given on very hot days and only in small amounts. It should also be supervised, I'm not saying stand there and watch until it's all eaten up, but someone should be around if your goat is being given a frozen treat to cool down.

Hanging bottle treat

Or you can make a treat bottle in the same way, with holes on the bottom or the lid left off and hung up. The goat will have to really work at it to make the treats come out.

Hay hanger

If you hang your hay in hay nets, try suspending them from the rafters so that the goat has to work at getting the hay out as the bundle moves and sways.

Grazing roller

Or you can tie hay around a drainpipe with strong jute or hemp string. Wrap a lot round and tie on great big handfuls of it. Then you can leave it with your goat to graze from. This way, it will roll out of reach, making your goat work a little harder for their dinner.

Obstacle course

Goats love to climb. It's obvious really, but they really do love to clamber about. Having lots of things for them to climb on is essential stimulation for a goat. It's also very entertaining to watch. An obstacle course can be made from anything that won't hurt them.

Seesaw

That's right. Many goats love a seesaw. A barrel with a plant tied to it will provide hours of fun, and when they're done playing on the seesaw they'll enjoy nibbling on the rope.

Dinner hanger

Handing their food is a great way to keep your goat entertained while they are indoors overnight. There are lots of ways to do this, but wrapping the regular feed up with a few treats and binding it in hay is a great way to do it. If you bind the hay tight with jute or hemp, the food will be bound up and difficult to get at, providing a little extra challenge with dinner.

Bobbing for apples

All you need is a large water container barrel and some apples. This is a really fun game for your goat, they can search around for ages and can be left to play with this on their own.

Home made feed-ball

Goats love to kick things about and you can use any large container such as a 2-litre drinks bottle or a gallon milk bottle to make your own feed-ball. If you drill a few holes in the side and leave the lid off you can fill the container with treats and leave the lid off to avoid choking. Your goat will love kicking this about and foraging for the tasty things that escape.

Play rope

The rope or string stays put and every day or every other day you change what you hang from the rope. It could be as easy and simple as a plastic milk jug, you can find some nice, hard rubber dog toys, and even plastic bowls of different shapes or colours. The ideal height depends on the goat's height. You would want to hang it such that the hanging item can just touch his back. My guys love to walk under some of the toys to try and scratch their backs & others they like to pull on. Some days you don't want to hang anything. The idea is to keep it interesting and see what you can come up with that is relatively safe.

Kick bottle

Bottles filled with treats make great kick toys. Just leave the lid off to avoid any risk of chocking on it and to let some of the treats come out. This should release the food only after some effort and scatter it randomly, encouraging natural foraging and grazing behaviour.

Rummage box

A rummage box is a spectacular idea for a goat toy. Take an old drawer or something similar and fill it with largish smooth pebbles so no noses or tongues get grazed. Then just pop in pieces of apple/treats in amongst the pebbles and the goat spends quite a while working his mouth around the pebbles to find the treats.

Paper bags/cardboard boxes

This isn't technically a made toy, but goats of all sizes love paper bags and scrunched up newspaper to make a game of. They toss them in the air and chase them and tear at them and have such fun! Boxes with any staples and tape removed are used much the same, but will last a little longer before they have been torn up completely.

Willow branches

Willow branches make great chews for goats. They absolutely love willow. Goats know what's good for them and willow kills worms and thins the blood, which stops it building up in the hooves. Thinner blood doesn't clog in the tiny capillaries in the hooves, reducing the likelihood of laminitas. Not only is willow good for your goat, but they love it too. Many riders include a willow stop on their route.

You can buy most of these things on eBay, but you can also pick these things up at supermarkets, second hand shops and scrap yards.

Chapter 10 Training your goat

Training your goat is a great way to spend time with them, to bond with them, and to save time and energy when it comes to doing routine things like cleaning out the feet, or unusual things like catching them for vet checks. And it can be done. Just look on YouTube for videos of clicker-trained goats.

The thing with training any animal is perseverance, but it is obvious from watching the goat wiggling its tail that they enjoy their games. Lots of positive reinforcement and the opportunity to exercise their brains and show off make training a great enrichment activity for goats.

The problem a lot of people have when it comes time to train their goat is that they don't want to give too many treats and make their goat ill or fat. This is where techniques you'd use for dog training come in. You can teach a goat to do almost anything with clicker training.

You need a clicker, which is a mechanical device that makes a click sound, and treats such as peanuts or flakes of cereal. By combining the click with a treat, you reinforce that the goat is doing the right thing. You need to start by getting the goat to make a connection between the clicker and a treat. To do this, click the clicker and then give the goat a treat about 20 to 30 times. Your goat begins to associate the clicker with food and eventually the clicker sound will be married up with the pleasure sensation from the treats in the animal's brain.

Coming When Called

Give your Nubian goat its clicker treat while saying its name over and over again. Do this daily to reinforce the training. Make sure that when goat comes to you, you do reward it each and every time.

Biting

If your Nubian goat gets into a habit of getting what they want by biting you, then they will continue to do so. If you pull away when your goat bites, then they will think they are in charge. They need to know that no one is in charge, but that no one is submissive.

The main thing to do if your goat bites is to understand *why* they have bitten. Could it be that they were just showing affection? In the wild, goats nibble at the top of each other's neck to show affection. Is it because they have been spooked by something and they are trying to get your attention or comfort? Or are they genuinely being aggressive?

If they are trying to show affection, you need to show them a more appropriate way. Teach them to show affection by nuzzling instead.

If they are spooked, put a firm hand on their neck and show them that they are safe.

If they are being aggressive, you need to be firm. Put your hand on their nose and push their face down –not so hard or firm as to hurt them, just enough to let them know that you won't stand for that sort of behaviour. Stand up straight and show them that you are bigger. It is important that you do not loose your temper at any point. If you loose your temper and make your animal afraid of you, it can take a very long time to regain their trust once you have broken it.

Showing hooves

Teaching your goat to be calm and stand still while you inspect each hoof will save time and reduce stress when it comes to checking and trimming hooves.

First, calm your goat, and stand next to them, still and firm. If there is anyone with you, ask him or her to calm your goat at their face, feeding them treats. If there is no one with you, stand your goat by their food trough, so that they are distracted and calm. The main event shouldn't be their feet being lifted and checked. If the most important thing that is happening is the food, then that is what they will care about. Hold the foot for a very short time at first, increasing the time as you go on. If you normalize the foot inspection by repeating this action as often as possible, then when the time comes to have the hooves rasped, cleaned out or trimmed there will be no fear involved.

Sit

Goats can be trained to sit much in the same way as dogs.

Teaching your goat to sit is relatively easy, especially if you have a particularly food-centered goat. Let the goat know that you have the treat. Let them know it's in your hand. Stand upright in font of the goat. Put the treat on your hand, palm up and move it above their head. The goat should automatically sit. When they do, say "sit" and give them the treat and a fuss. If they walk backwards instead of sitting, you could get someone to stand behind the goat. Repeating this whenever possible, without tiring out the goat, will mean they learn this very quickly. If the goat seems to be struggling with this, you can put a little light pressure on the back as you give the command. Do not push the goat's back down – this could not only hurt the goat, but break the trust. Training is about trust.

Lie down

Lie down, while not necessary, can be a really useful command to be able to give under some circumstances. With this method, you need to have already taught "sit". Get the goat to sit, but do not give the treat – keep it in your hand. Then point to or tap on the floor below the goats nose as they are sitting. The goat should lie down.

If they don't, you can apply a small amount of pressure on the shoulders, but not much. If you hurt your goat it will resent training and probably you. As I've already said, training is about trust. Once the goat lies down, say "lie down" and you give the treat.

Then, after doing this for a while, you can try saying the command and pointing before the goat lies down. Once they've got the hang of this, stand up and do the whole thing from standing until the goat has learned the trick.

Shake hoof

You can teach your goat to shake hands. It is easier to do this once the goat has learned to sit. Once the goat is sitting, take their front leg and give whatever command you've chosen. Then give the treat or the click. Keep doing this until the goat can remember to give the hoof on command before you take the hoof. Remember to reward every time they get it right.

Chapter 11 Breeding

As your goat is probably a dairy animal and you probably have her for milk, you will, obviously, be breeding from her. You will usually buy a goat that is in milk and then have to breed her once she runs dry, avoiding the drama of breeding until you are familiar with your doe.

If you own a male who is strong and healthy and are interested in hiring him out to stud, there is little to stop you. You should really seek advice from current goat breeders who have an excellent reputation with other breeders; check with your local goat association for more information. Most breeders will be happy to share information, as they're as keen as you to maintain high quality standards and to see more healthy goats.

1. Preparation

There are no different housing requirements, but you should be extra vigilant about hygiene and making sure the shed is cleaned out and free from anything that might damage a new baby kid. In case anything goes wrong you should have some colostrums in the freezer. This will allow you to get baby the immune protection it needs as soon as possible if, for any reason, the mother can't feed the kid.

2. Mating

If you've not got much experience with goats you really shouldn't attempt breeding at home. Take your doe to an experienced goat owner for stud.

Does can be bred when they weigh 85-90 pounds, usually at about nine months of age, but most people consider that you should wait a little longer than this and have the doe health checked before any breeding goes on.

Female goats are only receptive to breeding ("in heat" or estrus) for 2-3 days at a time, every 18-23 days or so, usually from fall to late winter. Signs to watch for include increased tail wagging, nervous bleating, a slightly swollen vulva, and frequent urination. Take the doe to visit the buck, record the date in your log, and watch for signs of heat again about three weeks later. If you see none the doe is probably pregnant.

Again mark your calendar, anticipating kidding about 145 to 150 days after breeding.

3. Pregnancy

You should make sure mum has a lot of good quality feed, extra grain and constant access to water. She will also need somewhere to keep warm and dry if the weather turns.

As soon as you know the doe is expecting, you should be observing her more closely.

About 50-100 days into the pregnancy you should stop milking (if you haven't already) and let her dry off. At this point she'll wean any kids that she still has at foot, anyway.

At 115 days, make sure she has enough vitamin E and selenium, and if you live in an area where the ground is deficient in these, give her a shot, your vet can advise you on this.

At 120-125 days give Enterotoxaemia & Tetanus vaccine; again, your vet will be able to advise you on this.

When your doe is 130 days gone, start adding vitamin E to the feed to make sure your kid is getting enough.

From 140 days onwards you should be ready for a baby to arrive any day.

Keep your fingernails short and clean – this isn't something you'll remember to do when the time comes, so just be prepped.

Shave her tummy and around her parts so that you can keep an eye on any movement. It also makes it easier to clean her up after the birth.

Start keeping her in the stall where she will be giving birth. If you only have 2 goats, just make sure their regular stall is clean and tidy. If you have a few, put her in a separate, clean stall with her 'best' friend- an animal she never fights with and who will keep her calm. This means that when the time comes, she won't be freaked out by being somewhere strange when she is in labour.

4. *Kidding*

Several days ahead of the due date, put the doe in a well-cleaned pen by herself with plenty of fresh bedding, water, and good hay. Don't be surprised if you check on her one morning and find her attending to 2-3 newborn kids, even if you didn't know she was in labour.

At the onset of labour she might paw the floor and lie down and stand again repeatedly. If she is in actual labour for more than two hours or seems to be having trouble, be ready to call for help from either a knowledgeable neighbour or a veterinarian. You should know in advance whom you're going to call. The best way to learn to deal with rare, difficult births is by watching someone with experience.

The normal procedure after kidding is to clear the nose of mucus or membranes to prevent suffocation (the mother will do this if you aren't there), disinfect the navel with iodine, and dry the kid. Gently draw a small stream of milk from each teat to be sure it's functional and not plugged. Clean up the soiled bedding and add fresh, if needed. Watch to be certain the kids get that all-important first drink of "colostrums," or first milk, or milk the doe and feed the kids with a bottle and lamb nipple. This thick, yellowish milk produced for the first few days after giving birth is essential for any newborn.

5. *Bringing up baby*

There are many theories of kid raising. The "natural" way would be to leave them with their mother. This won't work if you're raising goats for milk. Kids can ruin udders on show goats. And concerns about certain diseases (CAE) lead many goat raisers to remove kids from their mothers immediately after birth.

Be sure to provide fine-stemmed hay available to the kid, which kids will start nibbling at when they're only a week old. This roughage is essential for the proper development of the stomach and rumen. They will nibble at grain (18% kid ration) soon after, but the hay is more important. Limiting feeding milk at this point will encourage hay and grain consumption, but always offer as much clean water as they will drink.

Wean by weight, not age, usually around 20 pounds. The primary consideration should be whether they are consuming enough hay and grain to continue to thrive without milk.

Insurance

One thing you need to take into account is that your insurance may be invalidated by a pregnancy. You'd need to contact your insurer to find out where you stand. They might have a special pregnancy cover, but they might not. Just not telling the insurance company isn't really an option as someone would notice. Your insurance may be affected for some time after the birth as well. Most goat insurance will cover pregnancy as they are generally kept as dairy animals.

Dangers

There are all sorts of infections that can kill the foetus before it is even born. A dead foetus in the uterus can release toxins that can kill the doe. A pregnant doe can become erratic and her behaviour may change permanently.

Pregnancy of young does can hinder their growth, so you need to make sure your doe is old enough and big enough. Coming into heat isn't necessarily a sign that she is physically prepared to have a baby.

Multiple kids- twins or triplets – can weaken the doe a lot and you need to make sure that your doe has access to enough quality feed to avoid illness.

A prolapsed uterus can kill a goat very easily, and you should have a vet look at your doe to check her over, as it could take up to 3 weeks of care to nurse her back to health, and without this she could die.

If your doe is eating and behaving normally then everything is probably fine, though, as they are essentially prey animals, they tend not to advertise any potential problems.

Any number of complications in pregnancy or birth could do some real damage, or even kill both mother and foal.

Legal ramifications

You are legally responsible for the kid even before they are born, and you are legally required to provide adequate care for them.

Looking after mum and baby

Keeping the nutrition high and the wind out is the main thing you can do to keep mum and baby safe and healthy. You should watch the baby. They should be on their feet and feeding within 2-3 hours. The mother will be very attached to them very quickly and should provide any care they need.

If the kid is early, struggling to breath, took more than 40 minutes to birth, the mare won't allow the baby to nurse or they take longer than 3 hours to be born they may well be in trouble. At this point you need to call your vet for help.

6. What to do if the mother rejects the babies

If your horse rejects her baby you need to act fast. Without the protection of their mother the foal could die very quickly. Try to reintroduce the foal.

If this fails, or if your doe dies in labour, contact all of the horse breeders you can. Try to find a lactating doe to foster the baby. They will often take another mare's foal if the foal is abandoned.

If you cannot find another doe to feed your foal, you need to keep them as warm as possible. Luckily, goat's milk is quite easy to get hold of. Any friendly farmer or goat breeder should be able to help you get hold of goat's colostrums in an emergency, but if you've prepped properly you should have some in the freezer.

The milk should be warmed but not burnt and cows milk is not appropriate, even, as some claim, so called 'scolded' cows milk. This will make little foal tummies very upset. So you have your warm goat's milk in the bottle. Always feed your goat standing up, if they are lying down they may drown. Kids to be hand-fed should be placed in a well-bedded, draft-free box, preferably out of sight and hearing of the mother. They can be fed from bottles or pans. It requires time and patience to teach a kid to drink from a pan, but cleaning and sanitizing bottles and nipples is more work.

Most people feed warmed milk (a goat's normal body temperature is 103°) three or four times a day. Start with 12-14 ounces a day, for the first few days, working up to as much as 24 ounces a day by the end of the week, if the kid will take it. Some won't. If your kid isn't taking as much as this – don't panic. As long as they are taking almost this much, and are bright and alert, then they should be fine. By the second week this will probably increase to 36 ounces a day.

If you're worried, contact a vet. There is also loads of advice about this on forums and people will be happy to help you.

NEVER feed a baby if it is cold. This can kill the kid, putting all your hard work and heartache to waste.

Chapter 12 Goats, the law and insurance

Before you get your Nubian goat, you need to know where you stand with the law and licensing. There is no point laying out all the time, money and effort involved in starting out with these animals, bonding with them, etc, only to discover that you're breaking the law. You could risk having the animals removed.

1. What licences do you need in your country?

UK

You currently do not need a licence to own or breed Nubian goats in the UK.

If you are keeping goats on your own land it needs to be registered. You need a County Parish Holding number (CPH) to keep agricultural animals, and even if they are miniature, goats are still counted as agricultural animals.

USA

In the USA it varies from state to state as to whether or not you need a licence to keep or move your goats.

2. What are your legal responsibilities?

UK

Under UK law you are responsible for the health and wellbeing of your animal. You are responsible for the nutritional needs of

97

your animal.

It is an offence not to provide adequate food and water.

It is an offence not to provide access to shelter.

It is an offence to allow your animal to live in unclean conditions.

It is an offence to go away without making provisions for the care of an animal.

It is an offence to intentionally harm an animal or to knowingly allow an animal to come to harm.

It is an offence not to provide adequate veterinary care.

If you are having financial difficulties this is no excuse, but the RSPCA and PDSA may be able to help out.

USA

According to the animal welfare act of 1996, owners have legal responsibilities to their animals.

It is an offence to allow an animal to remain in pain.

It is an offence to deny, purposefully or by omission, access to adequate food and water.

It is an offence to cause pain or distress or allow pain or distress to be caused.

You must comply with humane endpoints. (Humane endpoints are chosen to minimize or terminate the pain or distress of the experimental animals via euthanasia rather than waiting for their deaths as the endpoint.)

Because goats are agricultural animals- even if you keep them as pets – agricultural laws should be applied to them. If your goat dies unexpectedly, you need to inform the authorities.

Chapter 13 Cost

Obviously, like any animal, there is an economy of scale, and the more animals you have, the less the animals cost to keep per animal. Many people feel the commitment of milking a goat or a cow is too great. Land availability will often preclude the keeping of a cow and this is where the dairy goat finds her niche.

Assuming your goat never has access to grass and hedgerows and that you are not providing fresh green food, we will look at the worst case scenario of having to buy everything from a supplier.

This is a broad spectrum estimate as there will always be variations on the theme such as whether or not the goat is in milk, in kid, feeding kids and providing house milk and so on, but we will look at this in depth in a subsequent article.

20kgs of good hay or a mix of 2/3 hay, 1/3 barley or oat straw per week: £3-£5, or $5-$9

Between 5 and 10kgs of proprietary goat mix per week will cost roughly £3-4, or $5-$7

One bale of bedding straw: £1.50-£2 or $2-$4. Total cost £7.50 - £9 or $12-$14 per week.

If it is summer with grazing this will be reduced dramatically, likewise if you are prepared to pick greenstuffs for your goat/s. For example, if you have a dog to walk then you might as well take a bag to collect edible weeds in for your goat, such as dandelions.

A lot will depend on your circumstances.

Fencing will not be a one-off cost. Goats destroy fencing. When you work out the cost of the fencing you'll be using, which will be £60-£300 or $100-$500, you should remember to put something aside for repairs.

Depending on where you get your goat and what type of goat you get, your initial outlay on the animal itself will be £50-£300 or $80 -$500. A doe with a kid at her foot will cost more than one who hasn't got any milk, though some people prefer to get their goat used to them before they use the goat to milk. A pedigree Nubian will cost more than a cross, even though a cross could be what you really want.

Chapter 14 Biology

Goats are split hoofed rumens that live on grassland and browse on other vegetation. They are considered to be small livestock animals, compared to bigger animals such as cattle, camels and horses. This said, they're bigger than micro livestock such as hens, rabbits, and bees.

The goat, *Capra hircus,* was one of the first animals to be domesticated, eight to ten thousand years ago. The origins of the wild goats, *Capra aegagrus,* extend around the dry hills of the Mediterranean basin, including Turkey, Iran and Pakistan.

They are primarily prey animals and large predators all over the world will have a go at eating goats.

Each recognized breed of goats has specific weight ranges, which vary from over 300 lbs for bucks of larger breeds such as the Boer, to 45 to 60 lbs for smaller goat does. Within each breed, different strains or bloodlines may have different recognized sizes. At the bottom of the size range are miniature breeds such as the African Pigmy, which stand at 16 to 23 inches at the shoulder as adults.

Feral goats are most common on rocky or hilly countryside in the semi-arid rangelands. These areas provide security from predators and disturbance by humans. Goats are not normally found on flat, treeless plains, but can be found on flat country with dense shrub cover.

Favourable habitat requires availability of shelter, surface water and an abundance of preferred food species.

In drier districts, all sexually mature females in a herd may come into oestrus at the same time and it is thought that this is synchronised by male sexual activity. This can reduce the effects of predation by having a glut of potential victims in the form of young kids all of the same age.

Females can begin breeding at 6 months of age or when they weigh over 15 kg. Males reach sexual maturity at approximately 8 months, but competition for access to oestrus females is fierce and it is unlikely that young males are able to mate until they become large, dominant individuals.

Females may become pregnant in their first year and can become pregnant again soon after giving birth, as lactation does not stop oestrus or pregnancy. Therefore, they can breed twice in a year, as their usual gestation period is only 150 days. Twins and triplets are common, although it is very rare for all three triplets to be raised to independence. At any time in the high rainfall zone, between 16 and 53% of females have kids at foot. The average litter size is 1.3 kids per female.

Goats reach puberty between three and 15 months of age, depending on breed and nutritional status. Many breeders prefer to postpone breeding until the doe has reached 70% of the adult weight. However, this separation is rarely possible in extensively managed, open-range herds.

In temperate climates and among the Swiss breeds, the breeding season commences as the day length shortens, and ends in early spring or before. In equatorial regions, goats are able to breed at any time of the year. Successful breeding in these regions depends more on available forage than on day length. Does of any breed or region come into oestrus (heat) every 21 days for two to 48 hours. A doe in heat typically flags (vigorously wags) her tail often, stays near the buck if one is present, becomes more vocal, and may also show a decrease in appetite and milk production for the duration of the heat.

The intact males of many breeds come into rut in the fall as with the does' heat cycles. Bucks of equatorial breeds may show seasonal reduced fertility, but as with the does, are capable of breeding at all times. Rut is characterized by a decrease in appetite and obsessive interest in the does. Sebaceous scent glands at the base of the horns add to the male goat's odour, which is important to make him attractive to the female.

In addition to natural mating, artificial insemination has gained popularity among goat breeders, as it allows easy access to a wide variety of bloodlines.

Gestation length is approximately 150 days. Twins are the usual result, with single and triplet births also common. Less frequent are litters of quadruplet, quintuplet, and even sextuplet kids. Birthing, known as kidding, generally occurs uneventfully. Just before kidding, the doe will have a sunken area around the tail and hip, as well as heavy breathing. She may have a worried look, become restless and display great affection for her keeper. The mother often eats the placenta, which gives her much-needed nutrients, helps stanch her bleeding, and parallels the behaviour of wild herbivores, such as deer, to reduce the lure of the birth scent for predators.

Freshening (coming into milk production) occurs at kidding. On average, a good quality dairy doe will give at least 6 lb (2.7 l) of milk per day while she is in milk. A first-time milker may produce less, or as much as 16 lb (7.3 l), or more of milk in exceptional cases. After the lactation, the doe will "dry off", typically after she has been bred. Occasionally, goats that have not been bred and are continuously milked will continue lactation beyond the typical 305 days.

Females that are about to give birth leave the group and give birth in a protected spot. Kids are fully active soon after birth, but most, although not all, are hidden by their mothers and visited only for feeding. A few days after birth they join the mother on her travels. Females may then remain separate from herds containing adult males for 1 to 2 months.

The mortality rate of kids from birth to 6 months is high. Natural mortality rates amongst older goats are unknown but assumed to be about 10%. Adult mortality rates, from all causes including hunting and harvesting are about 26% in temperate regions.

Wild dogs, foxes, wedge-tailed eagles and feral pigs are all predators of feral goats. Wild dogs are the main predators of adult goats and appear to affect feral goat distribution. In northern Australia, goats are rarely present unless wild dogs are absent or controlled to low densities. Foxes are the main predators of feral goat kids in eastern Australia.

Goat populations can rapidly replenish after vigorous control programs. High levels of removal of feral goats from a population may increase survival rates and result in a faster than normal rate of increase. Goats have the potential to double their population every 1.6 years in the absence of mortality caused by human control efforts and predation.

The increased demand for goat meat, especially in the United States, could possibly be met in part through improving reproductive efficiency in our herds. Reproduction efficiency is one of the most important economic traits in terms of livestock production. Maintaining good reproductive functions in the herd is pivotal to the success of any livestock production system. Productivity and profitability is measured by ovulation rate, conception rate, the number of kids born, the number of kids weaned and the frequency in which they are produced.

Aside from sampling many things, goats are quite particular in what they actually consume, preferring to browse on the tips of woody shrubs and trees, as well as the occasional broad-leaved plant. However, it can be said that their plant diet is extremely varied, and includes some species which are otherwise toxic. They will seldom consume soiled food or contaminated water unless facing starvation. This is one reason goat-rearing is most often free ranging, since stall-fed goat-rearing involves extensive upkeep and is seldom commercially viable.

Goats prefer to browse on vines, on shrubbery and on weeds, more like deer than sheep, preferring them to grasses. Nightshade is poisonous; wilted fruit tree leaves can also kill goats. Silage (fermented corn stalks) and haylage (fermented grass hay) can be used if consumed immediately after opening - goats are particularly sensitive to *Listeria* bacteria that can grow in fermented feeds. Alfalfa, a high-protein plant, is widely fed as hay; fescue is the least palatable and least nutritious hay. Goats should not be fed grass showing any signs of mould.

The digestive physiology of a very young kid (like the young of other ruminants) is essentially the same as that of a monogastric animal. Milk digestion begins in the abomasums, the milk having bypassed the rumen via closure of the reticuloesophageal groove during suckling. At birth, the rumen is undeveloped, but as the kid begins to consume solid feed, the rumen soon increases in size and in its capacity to absorb nutrients.

The adult size of a particular goat is a product of its breed (genetic potential) and its diet while growing (nutritional potential.) As with all livestock, increased protein diets (10 to 14%) and sufficient calories during the pre-puberty period yield higher growth rates and larger eventual size than lower protein rates and limited calories. Large-framed goats, with a greater skeletal size, reach mature weight at a later age (36 to 42 months) than small-framed goats (18 to 24 months) if both are fed to their full potential. Large-framed goats need more calories than small-framed goats for maintenance of daily functions.

Forums and other sources of information

Forums

http://www.goatbiology.com
http://www.thegoatspot.net
http://www.dairygoatforum.com
http://www.goattalk.com
http://www.dairygoatinfo.com

feed suppliers

UK

http://www.millbryhill.co.uk
http://www.gjwtitmuss.co.uk
http://www.ebay.co.uk

USA

http://goat.purinamills.com
http://www.hiprofeeds.com
http://ebay.com

Index

Ingram Content Group UK Ltd.
Milton Keynes UK
UKHW021310290523
422514UK00016B/270